Angel Hunter is a potential author from Rotherham, United Kingdom. She has written about life experiences and how it is to live through them. She loves Halloween, cosy nights in watching films, and reading. She is trying to create a difference and show people that they are not alone.

Angel Hunter

SOUNDNESS OF MIND

AUSTIN MACAULEY PUBLISHERS
LONDON · CAMBRIDGE · NEW YORK · SHARJAH

Copyright © Angel Hunter 2025

The right of Angel Hunter to be identified as author of this work has been asserted by the author in accordance with sections 77 and 78 of the Copyright, Designs and Patents Act 1988.

All rights reserved. No part of this publication may be reproduced, stored in a retrieval system, or transmitted in any form or by any means, electronic, mechanical, photocopying, recording, or otherwise, without the prior permission of the publishers.

Any person who commits any unauthorised act in relation to this publication may be liable to criminal prosecution and civil claims for damages.

A CIP catalogue record for this title is available from the British Library.

ISBN 9781035884087 (Paperback)
ISBN 9781035884094 (e-pub e-book)

www.austinmacauley.com

First Published 2025
Austin Macauley Publishers Ltd®
1 Canada Square
Canary Wharf
London
E14 5AA

S. Bullers (previous pastoral year leader), thank you for believing I can make a difference, and for helping to support me for the last couple of years.

F. Slack (current year leader), thank you for supporting me and giving me a reason to keep going.

Christopher, thank you for everything you have done for me – it doesn't go unnoticed.

Courteney, thank you for helping me reach my full potential.

And thanks for the people who have made this happen.

Nothing to Say – Angel Hunter

The day I met you, everything changed,
Days became brighter,
My smile became wider,
No one understands how much you mean to me,
Not even you,
Over time, my smile began to fade,
Days turned into weeks,
Time changed you,
You're the stranger I once knew,
I know it's a part of life,
To lose people,
I never thought I would lose you,
I have nothing to say,
But the feeling of my heart silently breaking,
I though you said you would never leave?
Every sunny day reminds me of you,
The joy you once brought to me,
You found better people,
Your home,
But you leave me here,
Still searching for mine.

Silent Enemy – Angel Hunter

If only I could look different,
Maybe I could be liked more,
The hurt in your heart when you see with your eyes,
Why did I look like that?
Your head starts to feel heavy,
Your heart begins to cry,
Why can't I look different?
Searching everywhere for your reflection,
Do I look ok?
You don't recognise that person in the mirror,
Finding any flaws you can,
Why does my hair look like that?
Why does my body look like that?
What is wrong with me?
The face you once couldn't reach the mirror to see,
Is now the face that makes your heart bleed,
The fear in your eyes looking at your reflection,
If only I could look different,
Would it solve all my problems?
Maybe in another universe,
I can believe what everyone says,
In this one, I never will.

Words as Feelings – Angel Hunter

Words can describe feelings,
But only music makes you feel it,
Music can express your emotions,
With only a soundtrack and a few lyrics,
As a saying goes,
'Music is therapy'
For some it's true,
For some it's not,
Some use it to understand themselves,
Every song has a secret meaning,
Deep meaning,
That can only be described through the lyrics,
Those lyrics form into feelings,
Feelings that will forever stay,
Feelings that describe your exact situation,
Feelings that make you cry or shout,
You feel understood,
Your favourite song creates tranquillity,
The break you need from the world,
Even for a spilt second,
Music is not just random words being sung,
It's the feeling you desire.

Pages of a Book – Angel Hunter

Have you ever heard of the quote?
'Readers live a thousand lifetimes',
It's true,
Every reader has one favourite book,
As their eyes glide across the pages,
Their minds become lost,
It's like a whole new world,
You forget your surroundings,
As soon as your eyes lock on a book,
You're living another lifetime,
Like a dream,
It makes the world interesting,
An escape,
It may not be real,
But your mind could make it seem like a reality,
A glimpse of how it could be,
In a different universe,
Words written in the pages,
And an imaginative mind,
Could get you lost,
In the words in a book.

Dark Peace – Angel Hunter

Every raining day,
Brings you peace within it,
For some it doesn't,
For some it does,
For me,
It brings comfort,
Like somehow the world knows how you feel,
When you are in the dark for so long,
It becomes your new best friend,
It brings comfort,
You know it shouldn't,
It could end badly for you,
But where else do you belong? ,
Don't find it to comfortable,
You might get stuck,
Every rainy day,
You comfort yourself,
It gives you peace,
Every midnight sky,
Gives you dark peace when it shouldn't.

Am I a Child? – Angel Hunter

Am I a child?
I don't feel like one,
I think a part of me died that day,
In that place,
Somewhere I'll never forget,
The constant memories,
The same situation all over again,
The feeling over and over again,
My child-self died that day,
Was I a child or a victim?
Trying to wash your touch away,
Knowing I never will,
I'll never be fully clean,
You left me with nothing but trauma,
The only way to get rid of you,
Is to scratch myself clean,
I can't do that,
I just have to accept,
You are forever the worst part of me,
Was a child or a victim?
My soul is left in that place,
And you still haunt me through memories.

Control – Angel Hunter

You think you have everything,
In the grasp of your hands,
When you don't,
No one can control anything,
And that's ok,
Some things you can,
Like who you date,
But some things you can't,
Like how people see you,
You can't control everything,
But you can control your life,
What you do,
And how you live it,
If someone judges you,
It's not your fault,
We are all different,
Life is not just about what you can control,
Or what you can't,
But is also about having fun,
And living.

Lines with Colour – Angel Hunter

The lines you draw,
When the world feels not enough,
Or when it feels too much,
When you put that pen on your skin,
Everything seems to go silent,
You don't think of the consequences,
Or how long it will last,
Just the lines you draw, gives you peace,
Even for a short amount of time,
You will soon enough run out of room,
The chaos in your head seems to die down,
Make sure no one else sees those drawings,
People might think they are for attention,
Depending on the pen, it may last a while,
Try not to scrub it too hard in the shower,
It might hurt,
When you start to see them disappear,
And the world feels like it did before,
You will crave the need to draw again,
This wasn't about drawings,
It's sad,
Because you know exactly what it is about.

Tell Me Why – Angel Hunter

Why are there constant thoughts in my head?
Tell me why I can't be normal?
All these people asking if you are ok,
But it's the only words you can say,
Tell me when I am in pain, I can't say,
What's the point right?
Why am I so complex?
Why am I so ugly?
Sat in a room full of people,
And still my best friends is the thoughts in my head,
Are you ok?
Yes I am,
Tell me why I can't just say I am not,
The thoughts begin to suffocate your mind,
A million thoughts all at once,
Feels like you are going to die,
'I can do this' even with tears in your eyes and a heavy heart,
Tell me why I am screaming for help and you can't hear me?
Tell me why it won't stop?
Tell me why?

Sunset – Angel Hunter

A part of me died with you,
The hurt I felt,
Watching you get embedded in the earth,
It makes you think,
Someone's life could be over so fast,
It makes you cherish life more,
Seeing the hurt in others,
Tears coming down their cheeks,
Realisation hits you,
You can't see them again,
No more conversations,
No more laughs,
It's just over,
Ever since that day,
When I look at the sky,
And the sun is about to set,
I know you're watching me,
I hope I am making you proud,
It's been years,
Every now and then, I hurt all over again,
But you never truly died,
Because you will always live within my heart.

Swallowed Feelings – Angel Hunter

When I feel like crying,
It didn't look like it,
When the tears start to form,
I swallowed my feelings,
I would have looked vulnerable,
Push it down into a pit in your stomach,
And put a smile on your face,
It doesn't look like it,
But my heart cries,
As my eyes are kept dry,
Be careful,
If you do it too often,
You're trapped,
Those feelings lock into your heart,
Your eyes will stay empty for a while,
Keep swallowing those emotions like a pill,
You won't be able to tell the difference,
The pit in your stomach will become clustered,
Even with a smile on your face,
It numbs you,
Swallowing those feeling deeper,
Makes your heart ache harder.

Soulmate – Angel Hunter

How do you know when you're in love?
Is it a thought?
Or a feeling?
How do you know it will last?
Or will it end in divorce?
There are so many questions,
You don't know if it's pure,
Or a joke,
But within you,
My heart found a home,
The home I want to spend the rest of my life with,
You're my home,
You're a feeling that makes my heart beat faster,
But also a though that stays in my head,
My love for you is pure,
I would do anything for you,
Even if you wouldn't for me,
Love is confusing,
You never know how it will end,
Or the encounters we will have to face,
But what I do know is,
You made me realise what love is.

Yellow as the Sun – Angel Hunter

I feel free,
Not a worry in the world,
Is this what the end of the tunnel looks like?
Finally to be at ease,
The trees blooming brighter than my smile,
The smile knowing I made it,
The vivid green grass,
Which once looked so dull,
I've never seen this part of the world before,
The bright yellow flowers,
They are as pretty as the sun,
The world looked so dull,
If you think about it,
It never really was,
You just never saw it any different,
Only the flaws,
Sitting on the grass,
I was once so repulsed by,
Now gives me release,
I met the end of the tunnel,
That I thought never existed,
With greetings of flowers brighter than the sun.

A Bird and Two Nests – Angel Hunter

All of you looked so happy in that nest,
Never would I have thought,
It was a lie,
Three birds that soon turned into two,
One bird took their baby into another nest,
Every so often, the baby would go back to visit,
The baby bird was so confused,
I mean if it was your circumstance, wouldn't you be?
Having two different houses to visit,
Packing the bags to stop over,
The talks about one another,
Is it as glamorous as you thought?
'But you get two of everything',
Yes, but no place felt like home,
The feeling of not being loved,
Like it's all your fault,
Is it as great as you though it was going to be?
Another bird appearing in one nest,
Watching as it tears one bird and your relationship apart,
The constant arguments,
Like you lost a part of you that once felt so whole,
Will that feeling ever come back?

Lesson Learnt – Angel Hunter

I have learnt my lesson,
I didn't know,
It would cost everything,
It all went so fast,
I felt like I had everything,
Had,
Past tense,
You don't realise how much something means,
Until you lose it,
I learnt that too late,
Please come back,
I can't stand on my own two feet,
I need you,
To guide me how to,
You were everything to me,
The problem is,
You still are,
It has been a year,
I have learnt my lesson,
I am haunted by you,
Instead of being with you,
Please come back.

Wrong Directions – Angel Hunter

Why do I feel so bad?
Pretending you're not dying,
When in reality,
You feel so close to death,
What is happening to me?
I have gone back to square one,
I should have seen it coming,
I wish I could go back in time,
To where I could see,
A light at the end of the tunnel,
Now I am wondering,
Was it a light or a warning sign?
Should I have gone a different way?
Maybe then I wouldn't have gone back,
Days just seems to be getting worse,
What is happening?
What is happening?
I feel like I am dying,
That voice in my head has controlled me,
I have no control,
Was it really a warning sign?
Was I going in the wrong direction?
Or is it just my fate?

Keep Going – Angel Hunter

When you're little and get a graze on your knee,
When your mum kissed it better and told you to go back and play,
You kept going,
When you're older,
Your mum seems to distance from you,
Your mum chose to love someone else,
Mum, I am scared,
Mum, I need you,
Where are you?
Mum, love me back,
She still chose him over you,
Are you proud of me?
I left him,
Mum, I still need you,
I forgive you,
I am sorry I wasn't enough,
I need to keep going,
Even without your loving arms to hold me,
When I fall back down.

Observations – Angel Hunter

As you walked by,
I knew something was wrong,
It's like I can read you like a book,
But I don't even know you,
It feels like I've known you for years,
I can tell something is wrong,
Your eyes say so,
Your facial expressions,
Your body language,
I see how you feel,
Like I know you,
But I don't even know your name,
Is it a talent?
Or a curse?
Is it a lie?
You only walked passed,
And it's like there's history there,
It feels like I know you,
Even though we are strangers.

Disordered – Angel Hunter

My heart is aching like mad,
Pretending everything is fine,
In reality it's killing you,
You feel like you can't control anything,
So you try in other ways,
Procrastinating my recovery,
Thinking you're not good enough,
I am so tired,
Not physically,
But mentally tired and unwell,
With knowledge that you need some type of escape,
What do I do?
Trapped in a recurring circle,
How am I going to be saved this time?
I am completely lost,
Where do I belong in this world?
What should I do?
I feel stuck,
Like I am not myself,
I have never been this person before,
Why am I so lost?
Will I ever be found?

Growing Up – Angel Hunter

Scared to be in the dark,
But it now lives within you,
Growing up is strange,
Your whole perspective of life changes,
Scared there is a monster under your bed,
But now the real monster lives within you,
I would use every birthday wish,
I want to go back before the world showed me true colours,
When the only thing to worry about,
Was the monster under my bed,
Growing up is strange,
You could never recognise yourself now,
The light that was within you shone,
Mine burnt out a long time ago,
Can you please relight mine?
That little kid was so full of sunshine and rainbows,
Now is filled of the truth of the world,
When did it all change?
Growing up is strange,
You never realized when life changed,
You just look back and think,
When did I grow up?

Hourglass – Angel Hunter

An hourglass has limited time,
Just like our life,
From the moment you tip it upside down,
The clock starts,
Until finally it runs out,
Hourglasses are just like people,
Some just run out quicker,
Some try to break theirs,
Just so it does run out,
Sometimes it does break,
Sometimes it doesn't,
And when it doesn't, you wish it did,
Others don't,
I wish mine did when I tried,
What's the point of having an hourglass?
Mine should have broken a while ago,
Instead, you are left with the memories of trying to break it,
I wish mine did break when I tried,
You are left with constant thoughts,
Would it be better if it worked and mine broke?
They always follow you,
The thought of wanting it broke and to let go.

Unknown – Angel Hunter

The fear of what there is to come,
The unknown,
Not knowing where it will take you,
But also,
The adrenaline,
The excitement of where it could take you,
All the dreams,
The unknown isn't just scary,
Or exciting,
It could be both,
Having no idea what could happen,
But wanting to know,
The one thing I do know,
Is no matter how it makes you feel,
Life is unknown,
You might predict what could happen,
But how are you so sure?
That's why,
You live life to the fullest,
Because you don't know.

Quietly Drowning – Angel Hunter

I fell into the sea long ago,
I have struggled to swim since,
Trying to get back to the shallow,
Instead, drowning deeper and deeper,
The water covered my screams,
No one noticed,
You will soon run out of energy,
The current takes over you,
You have no control,
Be careful,
You need to keep swimming,
Or you will drown,
Fighting with the current to make it out alive,
Or you could get a life jacket,
It depends if you can reach it or not,
No one realised,
Maybe no one ever will,
It might be better for the current to control you,
It's hard,
To live with a heart that wants to try,
And a mind that wants to die,
You continue to quietly drown till one wins.

To My Childhood Self – Angel Hunter

I am so sorry for what we have become,
And for what has happened,
We have had a lot of downfalls,
But we get back up,
We are not left out anymore,
But the way you felt,
Still lives with me,
If I could,
I would give you a hug,
Just to let you know,
It will be ok,
We might not be the best,
Or an actress like you always wanted,
But want to spread the kindness,
You're so full of,
You should have never felt like that,
For you,
I will try and make it feel better,
I wish I could tell you everything,
But I can't,
For you,
I will try and make your dreams come true.

Secrets You Keep – Angel Hunter

A million thoughts in your head,
Why am I so fat?
Is a constant one,
That mirror is your worst enemy,
Picking out every flaw you have,
Trying everything to cover them up,
Weight is one you can't hide,
The food in your stomach starts to disappear,
Do I look better now?
I can't stand up without nearly passing out,
At least I look better,
Looking in the mirror,
Why am I still fat? I haven't eaten?
Fun little walks turn into miles of aches and pains,
The desire to become thinner grasps your head,
The exercising every day,
The feeling of numbness and emptiness fills you,
At least, I am skinnier now,
Looking in the mirror,
I still don't feel skinny enough,
The things you sacrifice tolerate yourself,
The secrets you keep hidden,
Follows you with every mile you walk.

I'm Lost – Angel Hunter

I want it to last forever,
The joy music brings,
The happiness,
The feeling of being wanted and loved,
That's all changed when we turned seven,
That little girl began to crumble,
Her world was changing,
Wondering what you did wrong,
Everything got worse when you turn nine,
No more confidence; the bullying got the best of me,
Holidays with a broken family,
Harsh judgement on yourself when you look in the mirror,
That all changed at the ripe age of thirteen,
Lost in this big world and the constant memories,
Feeling lonely, surrounded by friends,
Feeling euphoric was her fate,
Wanting it to be gone,
That little seven-year-old girl was so confused,
I'm sorry I lost her,
I never found myself,
I'm lost.

Grief – Angel Hunter

Grief is a weird concept,
One second you're on top of the world,
Another, you're as low as it gets,
It's not a nice feeling,
You just want someone to understand,
Instead, you're left alone,
Some experience it from a loss of someone they know,
Some experience it from a part of them dying,
Denial,
Anger,
Bargaining,
Depression,
And acceptance,
It's all a repetitive cycle,
No one will understand,
I mean,
How can you grief if they're not dead?
No one will get it,
The thought of distancing from them,
Remembering memories as you walk past them,
The sick feeling you get looking at them,
I just want to go back to when I wasn't stuck in this cycle,
Wouldn't life be so different?

Non-biological Sister – Angel Hunter

You came into my life,
As a stranger,
Never would I have thought,
You would mean everything to me,
My best friend,
My non-biological sister,
You saved me,
In more ways than you will ever understand,
I'm lucky to have you be a part of my lifetime,
If I was in a room full of every person I have met,
I would search for you,
The one who was always there,
The one who never saw me as a bad person,
You will always be the one I look for,
At my worst,
And at my best,
You're not just a stranger that one day I decided to trust,
You're my sister,
I promise,
To give you the best,
Because you deserve nothing less.

Friends as Family – Angel Hunter

Friendships come in different forms,
A quality everyone should have,
Is loyalty and support,
You don't have to know them for years,
That doesn't matter,
It's the friends,
Who promise to be there,
Even during your downfalls,
To never leave your side,
Those friendships,
Will last forever,
If they don't,
It is for the best,
It's never easy to lose a friend,
But the true ones stay,
They become the family you create,
I have never been more grateful,
You showed me you care,
I promise,
To protect you the best you can,
You're not just my friend,
You're my family.

For Those Teachers (You Know Who You Are) – Angel Hunter

Thank you,
When I feel like giving up,
You remind me there is a reason not to,
When I feel lost,
You bring me back to earth,
You think you have never taught me,
But you have,
When my head goes too dark,
You help me find the light every time,
I always thought,
I am the worst person,
You don't know how much it meant to me,
When you saw the good,
Thank you,
You gave me hope,
The courage to try,
The will to stay,
Even when I forget,
You still remind me,
When I thought the worst,
You made me see the best,
How do I thank you enough?